JuSTin'S JokeS

JUSTIN FLETCHER
Illustrated by Patrick Tate

First published in 2011
by Faber and Faber Limited
Bloomsbury House
74–77 Great Russell Street
London WC1B 3DA

Designed by Patrick Tate
Printed and bound by CPI Group (UK) Ltd, Croydon, CR0 4YY

A CIP record for this book is available from the British Library

978-0571–28042–1

4 6 8 10 9 7 5

Knock, knock.

Who's there?

Boo.

Boo who?

Don't cry, it's only a joke!

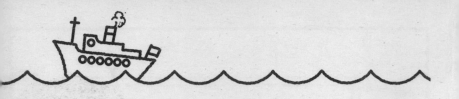

What do whales eat?

Fish and ships.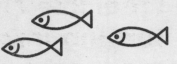

What is a pirate's favorite subject in school?

Arrrrrt.

Knock, knock.

Who's there?

Abby.

Abby who?

Abby birthday to you!

Where do rabbits get their eyes tested?

At the hoptician.

How do you get a baby astronaut to sleep?

Rocket.

What is the tallest building in the world?

A library – it has the most stories.

What do you call a man with a seagull on his head?

Cliff.

Why did Little Bo Peep lose her sheep?

She had a crook with her.

baaa!

What did the hat say to the scarf?

You hang around while I go on ahead.

What did the duck say when he'd finished shopping?

Put it on my bill please.

What do you call a joke book for chickens?

A yolk book.

$2+2=4$ ✓

$1+5=6$ ✓

Why did the teacher wear sunglasses?

Because his class was so bright.

What did the mayonnaise say to the fridge?

Close the door, I'm dressing.

What did the boy volcano say to the girl volcano?

I lava you.

What did the elf use to make himself taller?

Elf-raising flour.

How does a monkey make toast?

Under the gorilla.

What do you call a sleeping bull?

A bulldozer.

What did Mars say to Saturn?

Give me a ring sometime.

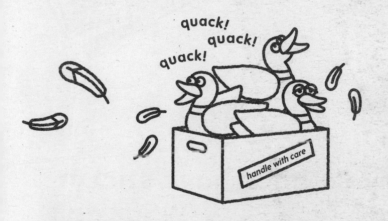

What do you get when you put three ducks in a carton?

A box of quackers.

What is a witch's favourite subject in school?

Spelling.

Why do bees have sticky hair?

Because they use honeycombs.

What do you call a fairy who smells?

Stinkerbell.

Where do you find giant snails?

On the ends of giants' fingers.

What's louder than an angry monster?

Two angry monsters.

What happened when the cat ate a ball of wool?

She had mittens!

Why couldn't the skeleton go to the ball?

He had no body to go with.

Why are fish so clever?

They live in schools.

When do astronauts eat?

At launch time.

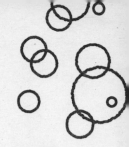

Why did the burglar take a bath?

To make a clean getaway.

Where do beavers keep their money?

In the river bank.

What do you call a pirate who's always making mistakes?

Wrong John Silver.

What do you get if you sit underneath a cow?

A pat on the head.

Waiter, do you serve lobsters?

Take a seat, madam, we serve anybody.

How do you make a sausage roll?

Push it down a hill.

What sleeps on the seabed?

A kipper.

What lies in a pram and wobbles?

A jelly baby.

Knock, knock.

Who's there?

Shirley.

Shirley who?

Shirley you haven't forgotten my name already!

What do cats eat for breakfast?

Mice crispies.

snap!
crackle!
squeak!

What do you call a man who doesn't sink in water?

Bob.

What's an ig?

An Eskimo's home without a loo.

Doctor, doctor, I've got a strawberry growing out of my head!

I'll give you some cream for that.

What do monsters have at teatime?

Scream cakes.

Why did the jelly wobble?

Because it saw the milkshake.

What did one bolt of lightning say to the other?

You are shocking!

What do you call a bee that can't make up its mind?

A maybe.

Why did the music teacher need a ladder?

To reach the high notes.

Have you heard the joke about the dustbin lorry?

It's a load of rubbish.

Why do birds fly south in the winter?

Because it's too far to walk.

To the South
500 miles

What is white and furry and smells of peppermints?

A Polo bear.

What's a flea's favourite way to travel?

Itch-hiking.

scratch

itch

Which cheese is made backwards?

Edam.

Why wasn't Cinderella any good at soccer?

She kept running away from the ball.

Why did the boy eat his homework?

Because the teacher said it was a piece of cake.

Which is the best day to go to the beach?

Sunday.

What did the sea say to the boat?

Nothing, it just waved.

Why is 6 afraid of 7?

Because 7 8 9.

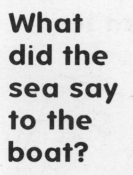

Which are the strongest creatures in the sea?

Mussels.

What vegetable needs a plumber?

A leek.

What is a crocodile's favourite game?

Snap.

Why did the wheel stop rolling?

Because it was tyred.

How do you know when an elephant has been in your fridge?

Footprints in the butter.

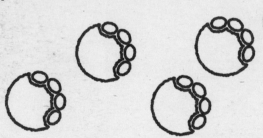

Who goes undercover in a bakery at Christmas?

A mince spy.

Why did the computer squeak?

Because someone stepped on its mouse.

eek!

What did one wall say to the other?

Meet you at the corner.

What time is it when an elephant sits on your fence?

Time to get a new fence.

What are an alien's favourite sweets?

Martian-mallows.

Where do sheep get their hair cut?

At the baa-baa's.

Who did the ghost take to the cinema?

His ghoul-friend.

39

Why do ducks watch the news? To get the feather forecast.

What did the left hand say to the right hand?

How does it feel to be right all the time?

How do you start a teddy-bear race?

Ready, teddy, go!

Which kind of cat likes to go bowling?

Alley cats.

mee-ow!

What has four legs but can't walk?

A table.

What did one eye say to the other?

Between you and me, something smells.

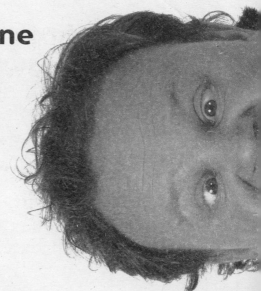

Why don't bats live alone?

They like to hang around with their friends.

Knock, knock.

Who's there?

Lettuce.

Lettuce who?

**Lettuce in,
it's cold out here!**

What's the difference between a guitar and a fish?

You can't tuna fish.

What's the best way to talk to a monster?

From a distance.

What animal can jump higher than a house?

Any animal – a house can't jump!

Why did the clown go to the doctor?

He felt a little funny.

What do you call a snowman in August?

A puddle.

How do you fix a broken pizza?

With tomato paste.

Why do potatoes make good detectives?

Because they keep their eyes peeled.

What kind of tree has hands?

A palm tree.

What is green and goes to summer camp?

A Brussel scout.

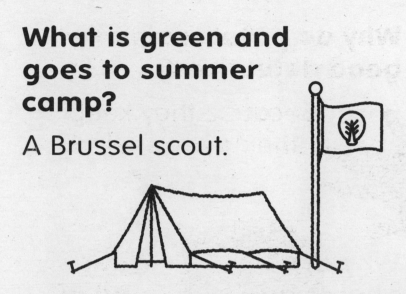

What do you call a man who spins straw into pudding?

Crumblestiltskin.

Why was the beach wet?

Because the seaweed.

Why are ghosts bad liars?

Because you can see right through them.

Which dinosaur is the noisiest sleeper?

A brontosnorus.

Why did the boy take a pencil to bed?

To draw the curtains.

mind that bee!

How do bees get to school?

On the school buzz.

What's the hardest thing about skydiving?

The ground.

Why do goats wear bells?

Because their horns don't work.

Why wasn't the moon hungry?

Because it was full.

What kind of shoes do frogs wear?

Open-toad sandals.

How do snails keep their shells shiny?

They use snail varnish.

Why was the piano outside the front door?

Because it forgot its keys.

How do you know there are three elephants in your fridge?

Because you can't shut the door.

What do you call a woman who stands between two goalposts?

Annette.

When is a door not a door?

When it's ajar.

Where does spaghetti dance?

At the meatball.

Why did the baby chick go to the pound shop?
Everything was going 'cheep cheep'.

What do you call a flying hippopotamus?

A jumbo jet.

Doctor, doctor, I feel like a biscuit!

That means you're crackers.

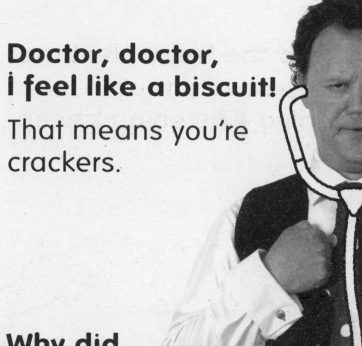

Why did the jelly bean go to school?

Because it wanted to be a smartie.

Why did the duck become a spy?

Because he was good at quacking codes.

What do you call a girl with a frog on her head?

Lily.

What does a bee say when it flies backwards?

Zzzb. Zzzb. Zzzb.

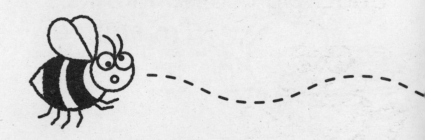

What did the big star say to the little star?

You're too young to be out at night.

What did the teddy bear say when she was offered pudding?

No thanks.
I'm stuffed.

Why did the cow cross the road?

To get to the udder side.

Knock, knock.

Who's there?

Peas.

Peas who?

Peas open the door and let me in.

What kind of onion likes to jump?

A spring onion.

wheee!

How does the moon cut his hair?

E-clipse it.

Waiter, will my pizza be long?

No sir, it will be round.

What do Santa's elves do after school?

Their gnomework.

65

What goes up when the rain comes down?

An umbrella.

Why did the king go to the dentist?

To get his teeth crowned.

What type of music are balloons scared of?

Pop music.

What did one magnet say to the other?

I find you very attractive.

Why did the teacher wear glasses?

To control her pupils.

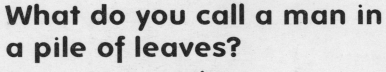

What do you call a man in a pile of leaves?

Russell.

What do you get when you cross an elephant with a fish?

Swimming trunks.

What do hedgehogs eat for lunch?

Prickled onions.

Why is it so hard to tell jokes to a snake?

Because you can't pull its leg.

What do spacemen play in their spare time?

Astronauts and crosses.

What do mermaids have on toast?

Mermerlade.

What's in the middle of a jellyfish's tummy?

A jelly-button.

Why did the spider buy a car?

She wanted to go for a spin.

What do you get if you cross a centipede and a parrot?

A walkie-talkie.

Knock, knock.

Who's there?

Ash.

Ash who?

Bless you!

How do you start a firefly race?

Ready, steady, glow!

What sort of fish would you find in a shoe?

An eel.

Waiter, what's this fly doing in my soup?

It looks like it's swimming, sir.

What gets wetter the more it dries?

A towel.

Why don't dogs make good dancers?

Because they have two left feet.

What do you call a man who walks all day?

Miles.

What kind of monkey floats through the air?

A baballoon.

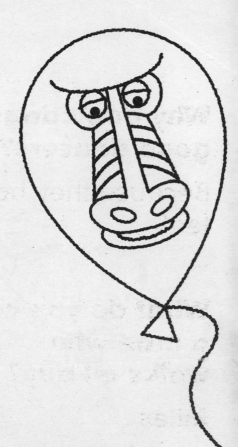

Which game do woolly mammoths like to play?

Squash.

What do cows dance to?

Moosic.

What do giraffes have that no other animal has?

Baby giraffes.

Why does Peter Pan always fly?

Because he can Never-Never land!

Why are police officers so strong?

Because they hold up traffic.

police control

**Doctor, doctor,
I keep thinking
I'm a bell!**

Take these
tablets and
give me a
ring in the
morning.

What do you call a train loaded with toffee?

A chew-chew train.

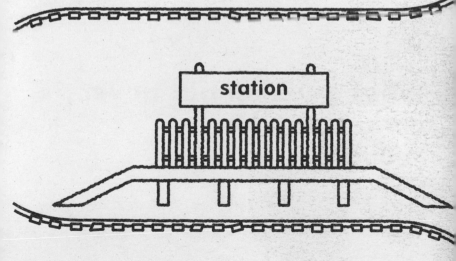

What has lots of legs and smells nice?

A scentipede.

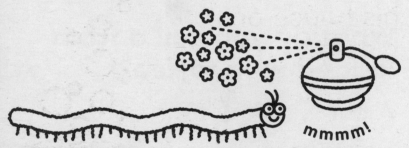

mmmm!

What goes up but never comes down?
Your age.

What is the strongest animal?

A snail. He carries his house on his back!

What can you hold but never touch?

Your breath.

**Teacher:
Can you name
two days of
the week that
start with 't'?**

Pupil:
Today and
tomorrow.

**What type of
nut doesn't
have a
shell?**

A doughnut.

What do you call a plant that grows out of your bottom?

Bum-boo.

Fifteen toilets have been stolen in a local village.

The police have nothing to go on!

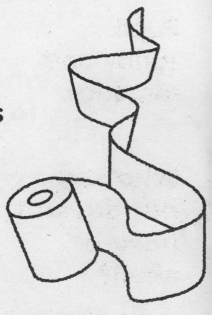

What has a head and a tail but no body?

A coin.

What is a lizard's favourite sport?

Cricket.

What time is it when a rhinoceros sits on your watch?

Time to get a new watch.

oops!

crunch!

Why are pirates pirates?

Because they arrrrrrrr.

What do birds eat for breakfast?

Tweetabix.

88

Why did the turkey cross the road?

It was the chicken's day off.

Ask Justin!

Do you tell jokes to your mum? (Eliza, age 7)

Yes. She has a great sense of humour but always tells me if it's not funny.

Do you like lions? (Rose, age 5)

Yes – especially when they roar with laughter!

What's your favourite dinner? (Peggy, age 6)

Cauliflower cheese.

What's your favourite joke? (Sylvie, age 5)

I've got too many to list here!

☆ ☆ ☆ ☆ ☆ ☆ ☆

What do you find the most handy things? (Oscar, age 5)

My computer and my head torch.

What do you want for Christmas? (Enzo, age 3)

A cocker spaniel.

JUSTIN'S JOKES

Justin Fletcher has worked as an actor, children's television presenter and voice-over artist for the past fifteen years. In 2008 he won a BAFTA for best children's television presenter and was awarded an MBE for his services to children's television and the charity sector. In BAFTA's 2010 Children's Awards, Justin's series **Something Special** won the Pre-School Live Action award, and he won his second award for best presenter. Justin's voice-over work includes the BAFTA-winning programme **The Tweenies**. He is also the 'voice' of Shaun in **Shaun the Sheep.**

Justin's Jokes is his first book.

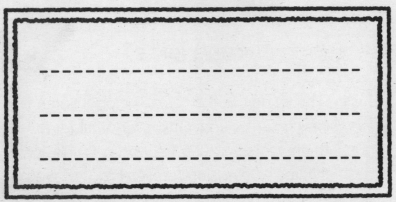

Write your best joke here!

- -

- -

- -

Send your best joke to **jokesforjustin@faber.co.uk**!
If we use it in Justin's next joke book,
we'll send you a free copy.

Terms and conditions apply. See
www.faber.co.uk/justinsjokes for details.